T0007718

Find the Truth!

Everything you are about to read is true *except* for one of the sentences on this page.

Which one is **TRUE**?

T or F Self-driving cars won't exist for another 100 years.

T or F Self-driving cars might help reduce pollution.

Find the answers in this book.

3

Contents

THE BIG TRUTH!

Technology company Google is leading the way with its self-driving cars.

Advanced computers can make driving decisions just as humans do.

A morning commute on a busy highway could one day be a great time to relax or get work done.

CHAPTER 1

Who's Controlling Those Cars?

It's 7:30 AM on a Monday, and everyone has a busy day ahead. Fortunately, people are able to make the most of their morning drive. A middle school teacher begins grading papers right after starting his car. Meanwhile, a bank manager reviews her files without even glancing at traffic. Finally, a dad dropping his kids off at school plays a quick game of checkers before pulling into the parking lot.

The average American spends about 38 hours per year stuck in traffic.

A New Way to Travel

How are all these activities possible—and safe? The answer lies in the future of self-driving cars. A self-driving car is a robotic vehicle that can travel without a human operator. These vehicles are also referred to as driverless cars or **autonomous** cars. In the years ahead, engineers anticipate that people will travel in fully autonomous automobiles that require no human **navigation**. Technology experts predict that such vehicles will be common on roadways within the next few decades.

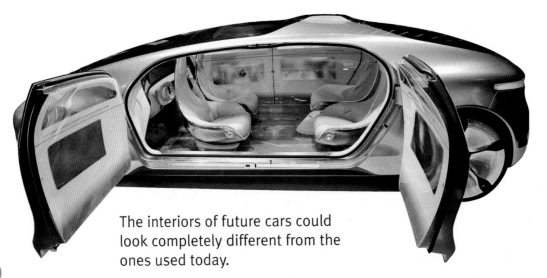

The interiors of future cars could look completely different from the ones used today.

Right now, drivers are still responsible for steering and paying attention to the road.

Adjusting to Autonomous Vehicles

Many people are already accustomed to certain automatic features in their cars. For example, most cars include antilock braking systems (ABS). This technology prevents a car's wheels from locking during braking and thus reduces skidding. In addition to ABS, drivers regularly use automatic features such as automatic locks and rearview cameras. But few people are familiar with vehicles that function without a driver to steer, operate foot pedals, or initiate turn signals.

Checking a phone while driving is extremely dangerous.

Amazing Benefits

It seems inevitable that fully autonomous cars will be the next step in vehicle engineering. Inventors are determined to produce self-driving cars that are safe and easy to use. Such cars could reduce pollution and make accidents less likely. In addition, people could be more productive while traveling. Because they wouldn't have to keep their eyes on the road, they would be able to get other things done.

Potential Problems

Engineers still need to address several important issues with self-driving cars. For example, some critics worry about what might happen if these vehicles were affected by a computer virus. And is it truly safe for drivers to give up control of their cars? As scientists work to answer these and other questions, the world continues to eagerly watch self-driving cars evolve into engineering wonders.

Engineers are hard at work testing and improving the latest autonomous cars.

Turning a crankshaft was the only way to start the earliest automobiles.

CHAPTER 2

Not a New Idea

People have been paving the way toward the development of self-driving cars since the early 20th century. Back then, drivers had to turn a handle called a crankshaft to start a car's engine. Moving the crankshaft by hand was difficult and time-consuming. But in 1911, engineers began replacing crankshafts with electric-starter motors.

The larger an engine was, the harder it was to turn the crankshaft.

A Look at the Linrrican Wonder

In the years that followed, inventors introduced several other automatic features that made driving safer, easier, and more **efficient**. Even as far back as the 1920s, engineers envisioned taking such technology a step farther. For example, in 1925, they tested a radio-controlled vehicle called the Linrrican Wonder in New York City.

By the 1920s, cars were becoming a common sight in busy cities such as New York City.

A man shows off a remote-controlled car in Washington, D.C., in 1928.

The first radio-controlled vehicle was a boat.

No one sat in the driver's seat of the Linrrican Wonder. Instead, it received radio signals sent by a second automobile that traveled behind it. These signals were used to control the Linrrican Wonder's electric motors. These motors navigated the vehicle. As amazing as this driverless car was, it was impractical to use two cars at once.

Decades ago, people envisioned autonomous cars that are similar to the ones being built today.

Built to Run on Special Roads

Though the Linrrican Wonder never became a popular addition to roadways, people didn't abandon the idea of self-driving cars. During the 1950s and 1960s, U.S. engineers experimented with driverless vehicles that were operated by **circuits** underneath the road. The circuits produced signals that controlled the cars' steering and braking. The disadvantage was that this plan would have required the rebuilding of most roadways.

Stepping Ahead With Sensors

During the 1980s, German researcher Ernst Dickmanns made an important breakthrough. He decided to add cameras and other sensors to a van. The sensors collected information about the van's environment. Computers then used the information to drive the van by controlling the steering and brakes. Throughout the next few decades, Dickmanns and other engineers continued to experiment with cars that required limited human control.

Sensors mounted on this SUV enable it to navigate without human assistance.

Improving Technology

Over time, self-driving cars have been programmed to change lanes, avoid obstacles, and travel extended distances. Today, car manufacturers continue to experiment with new technology. Inventors and engineers regularly add **innovations**, or improvements, that allow cars to navigate without human input. A fully autonomous car may still be a long way off, but the technology is advancing rapidly.

A vehicle designed by researchers at Carnegie Mellon University in Pittsburgh, Pennsylvania, competes in a race of autonomous cars in 2005.

Fact or Fiction?

Self-driving cars have earned a place in science fiction and fantasy. They've been depicted in literature and in films ranging from *Who Framed Roger Rabbit* (1988) to *I, Robot* (2004). Sometimes these automobiles are quite similar to the cars that real-life engineers have envisioned. Other times, they are far more fantastic than factual. For example, in Isaac Asimov's short story "Sally" (1953), autonomous vehicles "talk" to one another by slamming their doors and honking their horns!

Actor Will Smith emerges from an autonomous car in the film *I, Robot*.

19

Slippery, curvy roads were much more dangerous before the invention of antilock brakes.

Already on the Road

Many people feel like they are in total control when driving. However, today's drivers rely on more automatic features than they're probably aware of. Antilock brakes are one of these features. ABS prevents a car's wheels from locking up during sudden stops or when roadways are slippery.

 All new cars are required by law to be built with antilock braking systems.

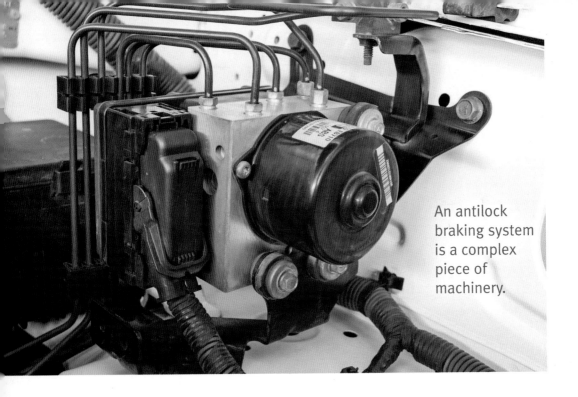

An antilock braking system is a complex piece of machinery.

Saved by ABS

If the wheels lock, a vehicle is likely to spin. This can lead to an accident. In a vehicle without antilock brakes, a driver avoids a spinout by using his or her foot to repeatedly pump the brake pedal. But in a vehicle with antilock brakes, a driver simply keeps his or her foot on the brake pedal, and the ABS pumps the brakes to keep the car from spinning.

Antilock braking systems rely on an electronic control unit of sensors and brake valves. The sensors monitor the speed at which the car's wheels are rotating. If the unit detects a wheel rotating slower or faster than the others, it signals the valves to apply and release pressure on the brakes. The ABS can pump the brakes up to 15 times per second! Meanwhile, the driver can focus on steering.

Backup cameras make it easier for drivers to safely back up their cars.

Ensure it is safe before maneuvering.

Setting the Speed

Adaptive cruise control (ACC) is another example of automatic technology that is found in many modern vehicles. With this feature, a driver sets a maximum speed at which to travel without using the gas pedal. As the car is in motion, the ACC's radar or laser system monitors driving conditions and adapts the car's speed as needed. The ACC automatically slows down or speeds up the car while maintaining a safe distance from other traffic.

A Timeline of Automatic Technology

1956
A rearview camera is featured on a car for the first time.

1985
Modern antilock braking systems are first used in cars.

Put Down That Map!

Navigation systems are yet another popular form of automatic technology in modern cars. They operate using the Global Positioning System (GPS). GPS receivers rely on **satellite** signals to pinpoint a vehicle's exact location. It can then provide step-by-step directions for reaching a destination. This makes it easier for people to concentrate on driving instead of reading maps.

1990
Inventors develop adaptive cruise control.

2000
Precise, reliable GPS navigation becomes available to the public.

Learn the Levels!

As the technology in self-driving cars has evolved, so has the language used to describe these driverless vehicles. The National Highway Traffic Safety Administration (NHTSA) has developed a system of levels to describe the different degrees of vehicle autonomy.

Level Zero: All Up to the Driver

At this level, the driver is in full control of a car. He or she is responsible for braking, steering, and accelerating. All early automobiles functioned at Level Zero.

Level One: Some Help Here and There

At Level One, some automatic functions exist to make a driver's job easier. For example, electronic stability control (ESC) is considered a Level One feature. ESC relies on a computerized system that can detect when a car is about to skid. It then applies the brakes in a manner that helps move the vehicle in the direction the driver wants it to go. Since ESC is required on new passenger cars in the United States, all new U.S. cars are described as at least Level One.

Level Two: It Takes Teamwork

To reach Level Two, a car must feature at least two automated systems that function together to perform a specific job for the driver. The combination of adaptive cruise control and automated steering is an example of Level Two technology. (Automated steering helps a vehicle remain centered in its lane.) A number of luxury cars currently operate at Level Two.

Level Three: On Standby

At Level Three, a vehicle is able to demonstrate limited self-driving capabilities. In other words, it is technically equipped to perform all major roadway operations. However, a human driver must be ready to seize control if necessary. Ideally, most of a driver's time in a Level Three car should be a hands-off experience. Nevertheless, he or she is typically able to take over functions such as steering, braking, or accelerating at any given moment. Currently, a small number of Level Three automobiles are being tested on public roadways.

Level Four: Total Technology

To reach Level Four, a car must be fully autonomous. Drivers using such a vehicle can input their destination, but the rest is up to technology. No one riding in a Level Four car should be expected to seize control at any point. Completely autonomous automobiles won't be available to the public for a while. However, they are already being designed and tested by various manufacturers.

Google is leading the way in autonomous vehicle technology today.

Google's cars have driven more than 1 million miles (1.6 million kilometers) as part of the testing phase.

On the Go With Google

Starting in 2009, the technology company Google began developing a **fleet** of self-driving cars. These vehicles are just steps away from being totally autonomous. They are already traveling along U.S. roadways. Currently, people who ride in Google's robotic cars are able to take control at any time. However, the automobiles mostly drive themselves. Riding in one of these cars provides an exciting glimpse into the future.

An Overview of Operation

Google's self-driving car operates by using a combination of cameras, sensors, radar and laser signals, and an onboard computer. Such technology enables the vehicle to create three-dimensional maps of its surroundings. The computer interprets these images alongside other detailed maps that already exist. The car uses the data produced by this process to navigate with limited human input.

Cameras are concealed in the front grille of Google's car.

Google's car is able to autonomously pass other vehicles and adjust its speed.

Google's cars are generally preprogrammed with departure and destination points. Apart from this information, the automobiles are designed to navigate independently. For example, they are able to determine the best travel routes between two locations. In addition, they can safely obey traffic signals, change lanes, slow down or accelerate, and pass other traffic.

A Google car demonstrates its ability to slow down and avoid cyclists.

Avoiding Obstacles

As Google's self-driving vehicles navigate roadways, they use sensors to monitor their surroundings. The cars' computers can detect and identify objects based on their size, their shape, and the way they're moving. This means Google's cars can sense if they are close to a **pedestrian** or a bicyclist. They can then react accordingly.

For instance, Google's self-driving cars would likely respond to bicyclists by moving away from them. They would also **yield** to people crossing an intersection. At present, Google's robotic vehicles are found mainly along suburban streets in Mountain View, California. This is where the company's headquarters is located. The cars are currently designed to reach maximum speeds of only 25 miles (40 km) per hour.

An early model of Google's autonomous car is parked in front of the company's headquarters in Mountain View, California.

What About a Wheel and Pedals?

At first, the self-driving cars traveling in and around Mountain View were also equipped with more familiar controls. People using Google's fleet of semiautonomous vehicles were able to grab onto a steering wheel or step on floor pedals to adjust the car's speed. They could immediately begin controlling the car if they suspected it wasn't working properly.

KEY FEATURES

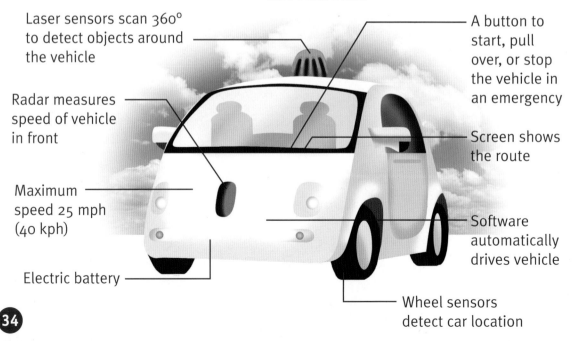

Laser sensors scan 360° to detect objects around the vehicle

Radar measures speed of vehicle in front

Maximum speed 25 mph (40 kph)

Electric battery

A button to start, pull over, or stop the vehicle in an emergency

Screen shows the route

Software automatically drives vehicle

Wheel sensors detect car location

Google's vehicle is equipped with a special button that can shut the car down if something goes wrong.

In 2014, Google took the next step by removing steering wheels and brake pedals from its cars. The main controls in Google's latest model are two buttons. One starts the car. The other shuts it down in case of an emergency.

Traveling down
the highway
could become an
extremely carefree
experience in the
near future.

CHAPTER 5

A Look Ahead at Autonomous Cars

As Google and other companies have already demonstrated, self-driving cars today seem less like science fiction and more like a remarkable reality. The idea that someone could safely work, text, or even sleep instead of paying attention to the road represents incredible possibilities. At the very least, fully autonomous vehicles would help people get more rest and be more productive.

Google plans for users to summon driverless cars using a smartphone app.

Autonomous cars could help cut down on traffic congestion in big cities by improving traffic flow.

Using Less Fuel

Self-driving cars could potentially serve several other important purposes as well. Some experts predict that such vehicles will result in more efficient driving and improve the flow of traffic. This means cars will use less gasoline. Because fuel contributes to pollution, this would benefit the environment, too.

Cutting Down on Crashes

Engineers also believe that fully autonomous cars will reduce accidents. Crashes related to **fatigued** drivers will be eliminated. In fact, experts have suggested that self-driving automobiles might save around 30,000 lives a year in the United States. In addition, it's possible that these cars will help prevent roughly 2.2 million vehicle-related injuries in this country annually.

Car crashes could become a thing of the past as self-driving vehicles become the norm.

More Mobile

Self-driving cars could be a game-changing technology for people who have trouble obtaining a driver's license. At present, certain medical conditions often require restrictions on driving privileges. Yet a person's driving abilities wouldn't affect the navigation of a completely autonomous vehicle. It is therefore likely that many people could rely on self-driving cars to become more mobile.

Blind people could soon have a much easier time getting from place to place.

Some people fear that the computers powering autonomous vehicles could be vulnerable to attacks from viruses.

Addressing the Issues

Despite the exciting possibilities of fully autonomous cars, engineers still need to address various questions and concerns. For example, some people are worried about what will happen if any equipment fails or if a virus infects an onboard computer. The scientists who are designing self-driving cars are still working on ways to deal with these and other potential problems.

Self-driving cars will need to be able to react quickly if people suddenly run out in front of them.

Costly Cars

Engineers also need to be certain that self-driving vehicles can safely respond to any unforeseen driving situations. Google cars, for example, have not been driven in heavy rain or snow. This means continued experiments and tests. Lastly, many people have pointed out that driverless cars will almost certainly be more expensive than traditional cars. The technology that makes these vehicles work will probably add between $3,000 and $10,000 to car prices.

Forever Changing Travel

Once self-driving cars are made available to the public, they will forever change the way people travel. Just as importantly, they will show how a vision of the future can trigger fantastic technological changes. In the course of a century, car technology has evolved from crankshaft motors to self-driving wonders that promise to reshape transportation. ★

Autonomous cars are a product of some of the most impressive technological advancements in automotive history.

Current maximum speed of Google's self-driving cars on public roads: 25 mi. per hour (40 kph)

Amount of fuel that might be saved once fully autonomous cars become available in the United States: 2.4 billion gal. (9 billion L) a year

Number of U.S. lives that might be saved once fully autonomous cars become available to the public: 30,000 a year

Number of U.S. vehicle-related injuries that might be avoided once fully autonomous cars become available to the public: 2.2 million a year

Amount that fully autonomous features will likely add to a car's price: Between $3,000 and $10,000

Did you find the truth?

F Self-driving cars won't exist for another 100 years.

T Self-driving cars might help reduce pollution.

Resources

Books

Dittmer, Lori. *The Future of Transportation*. Mankato, MN: Creative Education, 2013.

Gray, Leon. *How Does GPS Work?* New York: Gareth Stevens Publishing, 2014.

Visit this Scholastic Web site for more information on self-driving cars:

★ www.factsfornow.scholastic.com
Enter the keywords **Self-Driving Cars**

Important Words

autonomous (aw-TAH-nuh-muhs) — able to operate independently

circuits (SUR-kits) — pathways for electrical current to travel on

efficient (i-FISH-uhnt) — working very well and not wasting time or energy

fatigued (fuh-TEEGD) — very tired or weary

fleet (FLEET) — a number of ships, planes, or cars that form a group

innovations (in-uh-VAY-shuhnz) — new ideas or inventions

navigation (nav-uh-GAY-shun) — the practice of finding out where you are and where you need to go when you travel in a ship, an aircraft, or other vehicle

pedestrian (puh-DES-tree-uhn) — a person who travels on foot

satellite (SAT-uh-lite) — a spacecraft that is sent into orbit around Earth, the moon, or another heavenly body

yield (YEELD) — to allow someone else to move or finish doing something before taking your own turn

Index

Page numbers in **bold** indicate illustrations.

About the Author

Katie Marsico graduated from Northwestern University and worked as an editor in reference publishing before she began writing in 2006. Since that time, she has published more than 200 titles for children and young adults. Ms. Marsico would love to own a self-driving car that she could use to get her six children wherever they need to go.